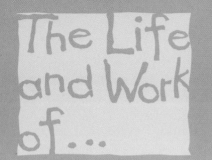

The Life and Work of...

Pablo
Picasso

Leonie Bennett

Heinemann Library
Chicago, Illinois

W9-AGD-635

© 2005 Heinemann Library
Published by Heinemann Library, a division of Reed Elsevier, Inc.
Chicago, Illinois
Customer Service 888-363-4266
Visit our website at www.heinemannlibrary.com

All rights reserved. No part of this publication may be reproduced or transmitted in any form or by any means, electronic or mechanical, including photocopying, recording, taping, or any information storage and retrieval system, without permission in writing from the publisher.
For information, address the publisher:
Heinemann Library, 100 N. LaSalle, Suite 1200, Chicago, IL 60602

Library of Congress Cataloging-in-Publication Data:
Bennett, Leonie.
    Life and work of Pablo Picasso / Leonie Bennett.
       p. cm. -- (The life and work of--)
    Includes bibliographical references and index.
    ISBN 1-4034-5072-2 (library binding) -- ISBN 1-4034-5563-5 (pbk.)
    1. Picasso, Pablo, 1881-1973--Juvenile literature. 2.
    Artists--France--Biography--Juvenile literature. I. Title.
    II. Series.

N6853.P5B46 2004
709'.2--dc22

                                    2004014059

Printed and bound by South China Printing Company, China

08 07 06 05
10 9 8 7 6 5 4 3 2 1

Acknowledgments
The author and publishers are grateful to the following for permission to reproduce copyright material:
AKG pp. 6, 10; AKG/Succession Picasso/DACS 2004 pp. 7, 17, 25; Bridgeman Art Library/Lauros/Giraudon/Museum of Modern Art, New York/ Succession Picasso/DACS 2004 p. 27; Bridgeman Art Library/Metropolitan Museum of Art /DACS 2004 p. 13; Bridgeman Art Library/Private Collection/Succession Picasso/DACS 2004 p. 5; Bridgeman Art Library/ Roger-Viollet/Succession Picasso/DACS 2004 p. 18; Bridgeman Art Library/ The Barnes Foundation Merion, Pennsylvania/Succession Picasso/ DACS 2004 p. 11; Corbis/Bettmann p. 4, 22; Corbis/Francis G. Mayer/ Succession Picasso/ DACS 2004 pp. 9, 21; Corbis/Kimbell Art Museum/Succession Picasso/ DACS 2004 p. 15; Hulton Getty pp. 24, 26; RMN-Beatrice Hatala/Succession Picasso/DACS 2004 p. 19; RMN-Michele Bellot/Succession Picasso/DACS 2004 p. 20; V&A Picture Library C.15-1958/Succession Picasso/DACS 2004 p. 23.

Cover painting (*Las Meninas (after Valazquez 1656 portrait of family of Philip IV of Spain)*, 1957) reproduced with permission of The Art Archive/Succession Picasso/DACS 2004 and portrait of Picasso reproduced with permission of Corbis ©Hulton-Deutsch Collection.

Every effort has been made to contact copyright holders of any material reproduced in this book. Any omissions will be rectified in subsequent printings if notice is given to the publisher.

Contents

Any words appearing in the text in bold, **like this**, are explained in the Glossary.

Who was Pablo Picasso?

Pablo Picasso was one of the most famous artists of the 20th century. He was Spanish but he spent most of his life in France.

Pablo Picasso was a painter, **sculptor,** and **potter**. He made thousands of works of art and created many different **styles**. This **cubist** picture has simple lines and blocks of color.

The Red Armchair, 1931

Early Years

Pablo Picasso was born in Malaga, Spain, on October 25, 1881. Pablo's father was a painter. Before Pablo could talk he drew pictures to tell people what he wanted.

When Pablo was only ten years old he went to art school. Pablo painted this picture when he was fifteen. His father was the **model** for the doctor.

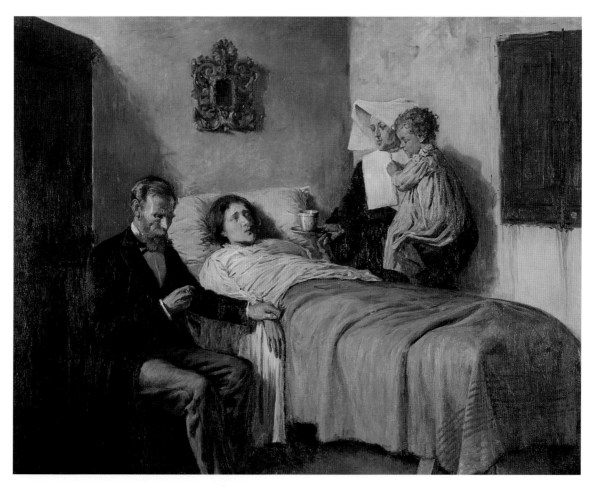

Science and Charity, 1897

The Blue Period

Between 1900 and 1904 Pablo spent a lot of time in Paris. A friend died and Picasso became very unhappy. He also was sad because he missed Spain.

Pablo's sadness showed in his art at this time. He painted people who had difficult lives. He used the color blue a lot. This is called his blue **period**.

The Tragedy, 1903

The Rose Period

In 1904 Pablo met a young woman called
Fernande in Paris. He was happy with her.
Now it was his happiness that showed through
in his paintings.

Acrobat and Young Harlequin, 1905

Pablo began to use pink in his paintings. This is called his rose **period**. He loved the circus and often went three times a week. He liked to paint circus people.

Masks and Statues

Pablo became interested in masks and statues from Africa and South America. He spent a lot of time studying them in museums. They were called **primitive art**.

Pablo sometimes painted people with mask-like faces. He painted a **portrait** of his friend, an American writer called Gertrude. She bought many of Pablo's paintings.

Portrait of Gertrude Stein, 1906

13

A New Style of Painting

Pablo began to work closely with another artist called Georges Braque. They tried to paint things from all sides at once. They called this new **style, cubism**.

In a cubist picture there are clues to what is shown. If you look carefully at this picture you can see a moustache, an eye, a pipe, and some fingers.

Man with a Pipe, 1911

Collage

Cubism was very **abstract**. It was hard to recognize the people or objects in the pictures. Pablo and Georges often met up to discuss their work.

They started making **collages**. They used newspaper headlines, sheet music, and pieces of wallpaper in their pictures. No one had thought of making works of art like this before.

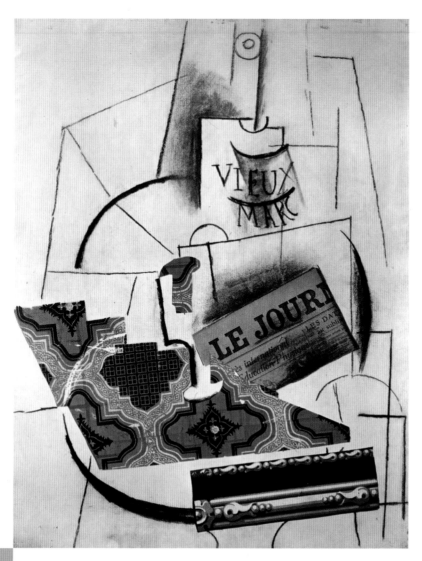

Bottle Vieux Marc, glass and paper, 1913

A New Type of Sculpture

Pablo made **sculpture** from things he found. At the time this was very unusual. He went for walks and brought back bits of junk that he stored in his studio.

Pablo put together different objects to make new shapes and forms. This bull's head is made from a bicycle saddle and some handlebars.

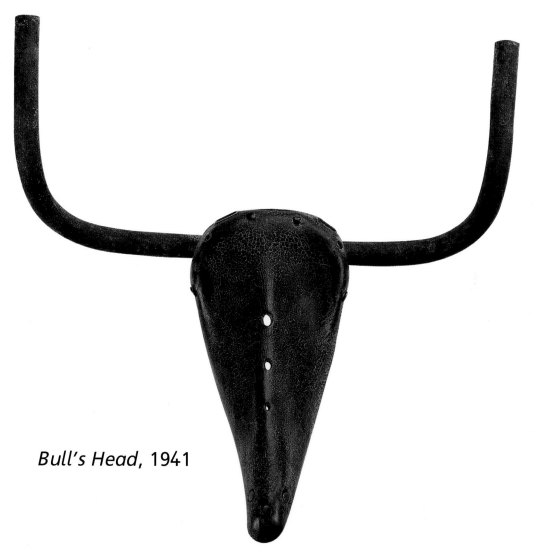

Bull's Head, 1941

War in Spain

In 1936 a **civil war** began in Spain. Pablo painted pictures to show how he felt about it. Here he is working on the most famous—*Guernica*. It was about as long as a bus.

Terrible things were happening to the people of Spain. Pablo painted this picture of a woman crying. It shows us how angry and unhappy he was.

Weeping Woman, 1937

The Potter

In 1947 Pablo went to live in the south of France. He had a new **partner**—Françoise—and they had two children, Claude (in picture) and Paloma. Pablo began a new type of work.

Pablo began to make **pottery**. He enjoyed it. In one year he made over 2,000 pottery objects. A lot of it was funny like this one.

Mounted Cavalier, 1951

An Active Old Age

In his 70s and 80s, Pablo was still making things and painting pictures. At the end of his life he painted three or four pictures a day.

Pablo had a new **model** named Jacqueline who **inspired** him. In 1961, at the age of 80, he married her. He painted this **portrait** of her.

Jacqueline with flowers, 1954

Pablo Dies

Pablo died on April 8, 1973. He was 91 years old.
He left us thousands of works of art. Many
famous artists who followed have learned from him.

Lots of Pablo's work tells how he feels. Some of it is sad. Some of it is angry. But lots of it is happy, like this picture of three musicians.

Three Masked Musicians, 1921

Timeline

1881	Pablo Ruiz Picasso is born on October 25 in Malaga, Spain.
1892	Pablo goes to art school at La Coruna.
1895	Pablo goes to art school in Barcelona.
1897	Pablo enters the Royal Academy, in Madrid. He paints *Science and Charity*.
1900	Pablo visits Paris.
1901	The beginning of Pablo's blue **period**.
1903	Pablo paints *The Tragedy*.
1904	Pablo settles in Paris and meets Fernande.
1905	The beginning of Pablo's rose period. Pablo paints *Acrobat and Young Harlequin*.
1906	Pablo paints **Portrait** *of Gertrude Stein*.
1907	Pablo meets Georges Braque and they begin to develop **cubism**.
1911	Pablo paints *Man with a Pipe*.
1913	Pablo makes collage *Bottle Vieux Marc, glass, and paper*.
1914	World War I begins.
1918	Pablo marries a Russian dancer called Olga. World War I ends.
1921	Pablo paints *Three Masked Musicians*. His first child, Paul, is born.
1925	Pablo takes part in the first **surrealist** exhibition.
1931	Pablo paints *The Red Armchair*.

1932	Pablo has a new **model** called Marie-Therese Walter.
1935	Pablo's second child, Maya, is born.
1936	The Spanish **Civil War** begins.
1937	Pablo paints *Guernica* and *Weeping Woman*.
1939	The Spanish Civil War ends.
	World War II begins. Pablo spends most of it in Paris.
1941	Pablo makes the **sculpture** *Bull's Head*.
1943	Pablo meets Françoise Gilot.
1945	World War II ends.
1947	Pablo goes to live in the south of France and makes lots of **pottery**. Pablo's son Claude is born.
1949	Pablo's fourth child, Paloma, is born.
1951	Pablo makes the pottery figure *Mounted Cavalier*.
1954	Pablo paints a portrait of Jacqueline Roque, called *Jacqueline with flowers*.
1961	Pablo marries Jacqueline.
1973	Pablo dies on April 8.

Glossary

abstract art that deals with ideas rather than the way things look

civil war war between people of the same country

collage picture made with paper, wood, or other materials as well as paint

cubism style of painting that shows objects from all sides at once

Guernica town in northern Spain that was badly bombed in 1937

inspire to help someone to be creative

model person who an artist paints or draws

partner person one lives with as if they were a husband or wife

period an amount of time

portrait a picture of a person

potter someone who makes things from clay, usually pots

primitive art art of native people of Africa, Latin America, and the Pacific, often made for religious reasons

sculptor an artist who makes art that is not flat—often made of wood, stone, or metal

sculpture a piece of art made by a sculptor

style the way something looks or is done

surrealist an artist who does work that is dream-like, using objects in an unexpected way

Find Out More

Paintings and sculptures to see

Painting. *Gertrude Stein*. 1906. The Metropolitan Museum of Art, New York.

Sculpture. *Head of a Woman*. 1909. Museum of Fine Arts, Boston.

Painting. *Daniel-Henry Kahnweiler*. 1910. The Art Institute of Chicago.

Painting. *Pierrot and Harlequin*. 1920. National Gallery of Art, Washington, D.C.

Painting. *Mandolin and Guitar*. 1924. Guggenheim Museum, New York.

Books to read

Shelly Swanson Sateren. *Masterpieces—Artists and Their Works: Picasso*. Mankato, Minnesota: Capstone Press, 2002.

Juliet Haslewood. *Introducing Picasso*. London, UK: Chrysalis Children's Books, 2002.

Linda Lowery. *On my Own: Pablo Picasso*. Minneapolis, Minnesota: Lerner Publishing Group, 1999.

Index